D1480363

And Peace at the Last

Christians Talk about Death

And Peace at the Last

Christians Talk about Death

Russell L. Dicks

Thomas S. Kepler

Evangel
Publishing House

Publisher's Cataloging-in-Publication Data
(Provided by Quality Books, Inc.)

Dicks, Russell L. (Russell Leslie), 1906–
    And peace at the last : Christians talk about death /
Russell L. Dicks, Thomas S. Kepler.
    p. cm.

    LCCN 2004100416
    ISBN 1-928915-55-8

    1. Death—Religious aspects—Christianity.
    2. Terminally ill—Prayer-books and devotions—English.
    I. Kepler, Thomas S. (Thomas Samuel) 1897– II. Title.

BT825.D53 2004   236'.1
                                  QBI04-200056

Printed in the United States of America
5 4 3 2

Table of Contents

Preface

This book is written for those who like to plan their lives ahead so that the inevitable does not overtake them unprepared. It also is written for those who are near the time of death and would welcome help in passing through the experience of dying.

Many do not dread death as such, but they do dread the experience of dying. Medical science is making marked strides in taking the pain out of suffering through its use of drugs and surgery, but there still remains the emotional acceptance of the experiences of dying and death. This calls for spiritual insight, and it is with this phase of the subject that this book deals.

The book is divided into two parts. Part I deals with the experience of dying, Part II with death. Part I presents the imaginary story of a person who is going through the experience and deals with such topics as the patient's resentments, anxieties, hopes, and faith. It shows him seeking inner resources and presents specific ways in which he seeks to maintain his poise. Here we discuss the role of the physician, the pastor, the family, and friends. Whimsy, humor, and the light touch are utilized deliberately. Part I is based upon my approximately twenty years of close and intimate ministry to dying people as a hospital chaplain. Just how many people I have stood beside as they discussed this subject or sat beside as they waited out this experience, I have no way of knowing, but the number has been large.

Part II draws upon the wisdom and conviction of other writers, both ancient and modern, concerning this subject. And who would be better prepared to glean pertinent material for our day than Dr. Thomas S. Kepler? Dr. Kepler is a professor of New Testament and the author of numerous books about the deep things of the spirit.

It is my personal belief that much of the increase of anxiety in our times, which is incapacitating large numbers of people, can be traced to a failure to accept the reality of death. This theory neither can be proved nor disproved, but many observers of human life today would support it.

I further believe that the human creature is capable of a heroic death. While most people die commonplace deaths, little realizing and seemingly not caring what is happening to them, this need not be. In large part, the Protestant church has stopped talking about this subject because pastors and parishioners alike reject a sentimental approach to death. This is all the more reason to throw the spotlight upon the subject.

— RUSSELL L. DICKS

Part I

An Experience of Dying

1. Discovery

Last night I died. My death was not unexpected, for I have been ill for some time. I died at home in my own bed.

Someone once said to Robert Browning, "Robert, you'll die in a dress suit." William Lyon Phelps of Yale University observed that Browning didn't do that, but "he died in bed like a Christian." Such was my death.

I have known I would not recover for some three months; the last two I have been confined to my room and my bed. Some time ago I inquired of my doctor about my condition. At first he gave me an evasive answer. Having been around doctors a great deal and understanding their tendency to overprotect their patients (which is desirable with most people, I suppose), I asked him more directly.

"Now, Fred," I said, "I know you would like to help me, and you have. I depend upon your skill and your good judgment, but I don't want you to keep me guessing and wondering. How much time do you think I'll have?"

He took a deep breath, pulled up a chair, and sat down beside me. He said: "You and I have been friends a long time. I knew you would want to know sooner or later, and I told your wife that I would tell you when you asked."

"How long has she known?"

"About two months."

"I'm sorry she had to carry it that long alone. How much time yet?"

"I don't know for certain, of course — three months, six, not over eight at the most."

"Three to eight months — well, that makes it pretty definite, even though there's a five months' leeway."

"We can't be too definite, you know, and then it's not good to be counting the days. You know that."

"Yes, I'm sure one shouldn't count the days, and I have no intention of doing so," I replied. "You'll be able to keep me comfortable?"

"Yes, there are a lot of things we can do now to relieve pain. You'll have some, but how much I don't know."

"You've told my wife, you said."

"Yes, I told her soon after I knew. Want me to tell her we've talked about it?"

"Not for a couple of days. I'd like to have a little time with it before we talk."

"Okay. I hoped you'd take it this way."

I shrugged my shoulders. "How else can I take it?" My voice was tinged with bitterness, which he ignored. I added, "Thanks for telling me, Fred." With that he left.

I lay looking out the window, looking at nothing in particular. Various thoughts pushed into my mind, seeking to claim my attention, but none of them succeeded for long.

A slow, creeping bitterness seemed to lay hold upon me, and I wanted to blame someone—but whom? My doctor came to my mind. Why hadn't he been able to do something? Medical science was always doing the unexpected. Why couldn't the doctor help me? Then I remembered several times during my life when doctors had relieved my suffering and, upon two occasions at least, had prevented my death. Also, I had known many who died far more tragic deaths than mine would be, for I had been able to provide reasonably well for my family. So why blame the doctor? Rather, I could be thankful for a man like him who had the courage to be honest with me.

Could I blame my family, because of the demands they had made upon me? Of course not. To have cared for them and shared with them in the adventure of life was a privilege that did not come to all men.

What about those with whom I had worked? They often had made unreasonable demands upon me. No, of course I couldn't blame them.

That left only God. I could blame Him, as some people do. I laughed an embarrassed and self-conscious laugh. That would be false to my deepest convictions, for I often had spoken out against people's tendency to blame God for anything they cannot understand.

Then I thought of what a physician had told me about a Southern family whom he was serving. Death had come to the father of the family and, as the doctor entered the room, the family was gathered around the bed. An atmosphere of near hysteria filled the room. Then an old black woman who had served the family for many years came into the room, saying in a chantlike voice as she knelt at the foot of the bed, "The Lord has given and the Lord has taken away. Blessed be the name of the Lord." Immediately, the doctor reported, a quiet dignity came into the room that had not been present before.

People have believed that since the dawn of history: The Lord gives and the Lord takes away. As I had often said, however, God probably is not so much concerned about *when* we die; He is certainly concerned about *how* we die. I had said that before congregations and classes of theological students repeatedly, and now that it was soon to come to me—*how* would I die? Now I would have a chance to demonstrate the truth of my beliefs. I knew that many persons worry not so much about death, but about the way they will die. They wonder whether they will be able "to die like a man," as one fellow put it.

I lay reflecting, suddenly conscious that my early resentment had passed. I was a little surprised to realize that my mind still worked as it was accustomed to. The moments passed, the clock chimed, the telephone downstairs rang. In the distance I could hear my wife's voice faintly: "Yes, he had a pretty good night. Yes, the doctor was here this morning. I'm sure he would like to see you this afternoon after his rest hour for a short time. He's working a little, but come about four if you can."

Now who was that? I wondered. *Why had she told him to come without asking me?* I couldn't see anyone now—she should know that. I had a great deal of work to do. Work . . . all my life I had given first attention to my work; it now seemed oddly unimportant. Why? If it was important yesterday, it was important today. And, of course, I would see whomever wanted to come. I picked up my pen, but my thoughts trailed off.

It will soon be over, I reflected. I had been so preoccupied with the work, the worry, the concern about many things, most of which now seemed relatively insignificant. Suddenly, I wished I had done fewer things and had done them better. It would have been a better use of time.

Time . . . what is time? Now I seemed to have so little of it. Three months, the doctor had said, but maybe it would be longer. If I tried, perhaps I could stretch it to the upper limit of eight months. But why struggle for more time? What would I do with it? Perhaps I could help someone a little, write a few more articles, enjoy companionship with those I loved that much longer. . . . Then I thought of the time I had wasted by failing to express my affection for them in the past. There it was again: regret at wasted time. What about other regrets? Regret concerning misjudgments and misdirected efforts: sins, some would call them. Oh, I'd had plenty of those, but they all seemed pretty vague and far removed now. I had hurt my share of people, some pretty badly, and I had done my share of hating. A slow surge of anger rose in my mind at the thought of two or three experiences in which I had been helpless in the face of circumstances. I thought, *There are some people who are just plain skunks. . . .*

A spasm of pain slowly moved through my body—set off, I realized, by the anger that had filled my mind. *They still hurt me, those underhanded skunks. . . .* When I got relaxed, after I had wiped the perspiration from my face, I determined not to let that happen again. I always had hoped to repay their treachery with good measure; but the years had passed, they had prospered, and the opportunity had never presented itself. Now my time was drawing to an end. What was the sense of worrying about it? The thought occurred to me that I should forgive them, but it was immediately rejected as juvenile. They would laugh at me; after all, it was a part of the struggle. One had his own life to live and mine was nearly finished.

I lay back and closed my eyes. The morning had tired me more than I realized, but at least I now knew where I stood. For several weeks doubts about my recovery had been creeping into my mind and disturbing me. That was why I had asked Fred to come this morning; he ordinarily came in the afternoon. Mornings always had been my best time, when my mind was clearest and I could do my best thinking. Now the morning was nearly past, and with it all the mornings as I had known them. What I needed was a plan, an outline, such as I had prepared for my books. Well, that could come later. Now I needed to rest, to relax, to let the tension and fatigue flow from me and the quietness of God flow into me.

"In quietness and in confidence shall be your strength" (Isa. 30:15, KJV).
Quietness, the quietness of God.

The quietness that comes when the mind
    is still,
When its tensions have flown out of one.
Quietness waits for the spirit as the
    spring earth waits for the rain;
And the sun upon it, and the spark of life
    within it.
I thought of the slow turning of the soil in
    the spring,
The harrowing, the planting, and the
    waiting for the first tender shoots to
    thrust their heads above the soil:
Their growth a mystery, a mystery of life.
"In quietness and in confidence shall be
    your strength":
The quietness is the planting and confi-
    dence is the growth,
The sure growth that fills the earth;
At all times and in all things:
The growth of a plant from a seed,
The growth of a fowl from an egg,
The growth of a person from a tiny,
    helpless, scrawny baby.
Quietness is the brooding, the planning,
    the reflection;
Confidence is the courage that carries the
    plans through to completion;
Quietness creates the blueprints;
Confidence builds the building;
Quietness charts the way,

Confidence follows the course.
"In quietness and in confidence shall be
your strength."
I will rest in quietness and confidence
And they will support me. . . .

My mind trailed off into sleep. My wife tip-
toed into the room. I knew she was there, but I
did not stir, for I was at rest in quietness and
peace and hope.

2. Memories

My first experience with death came at the age of ten when my father, after an illness of twelve weeks, died at three o'clock one morning. An aunt roused me from sleep and helped me to get dressed. Then, as we stood in my father's bedroom, listening to my mother's steady sobs, my aunt stood with her arm around me and whispered: "Look at your father. It is the last time you will ever see him alive."

The memory of his illness came back to me now, as I lay thinking about death and what I knew about it, since I had recently learned that I soon would face it myself. We were living on a farm, and the neighbors had shared the nursing care of my father. I remembered my mother's hurried preoccupation and my older brother's heavy mood. No one had paid much attention to me except to shoo me out of the way and send me after more wood for the wood box, for it was February and the fires burned day and night. As the wood pile dropped, two wagonloads of poles were added and then hastily cut up one afternoon by two neighbors and their strong-backed, noisy sons. That day they seemed curiously sober and had treated me quite differently from the rowdy way they ordinarily used with me. But the wood box behind the stove seemed constantly empty, and I was often hungry because no one bothered to prepare meals except for my father. I had wondered when the others ate, especially my mother. She caught me in her arms one day, with an unusual expression of affection on her face, and cried, "You poor orphan, whatever will become of you?" I had been embarrassed and baffled and had cried myself to sleep that night. A curious resentment built up inside me toward my father.

I must be careful that my own illness not become so demanding that the usual needs of those around me are overlooked, I reflected. Soon I must have a talk with my wife about these things and about her own attitudes. She would have the hardest time of all, for others were busy with their own plans; that's the way it usually is with the younger generations, and that's the way it should be. Of course, one heard of the exceptions: the son so devoted to his mother, the daughter tied so closely to her father that both children were emotionally handicapped persons who found it impossible to take up their lives away from the family.

I wondered if my wife would remarry. That was not a pleasant thought. But then, why not? One ought to be mature about such things. Why shouldn't she remarry? Marriage was companionship, basically, and she'd need companionship. It actually would be her own problem, but I should discuss it with her, perhaps free her emotionally from some of my domination. She might give herself a chance to enter a new relationship more readily if she knew I wanted her to. . . .

I sat wondering, feeling rather uncomfortable as these thoughts passed through my mind. Then I realized, with something of a shock, that my desire for such a conversation with her was an effort to project myself into whatever relationship she might develop. *That would be very unfair to her and unfair to whoever might become interested in her,* I thought. Then I realized I was deliberately avoiding thinking of the word, *love.* I couldn't imagine how she could "fall in love" with anyone else; it would be a friendship. I smiled. *Now, there is a good example of the male ego in operation! Why* couldn't *she have a love relationship with someone else? Other people did. But ours had been such a satisfying love for each other.* I supposed everybody would think this under similar circumstances.

What she did after I was gone was strictly her own affair, and I had no business trying to interfere. *Well, anyway,* I smiled somewhat sardonically, *she would have a hard time finding anybody to fill my shoes — if for no other reason, because she was used to me.* At least I could be certain of that.

The idea of being concerned about whether my wife would remarry after my death struck me as curious. What ridiculous things we think up to worry about! A minister once had consulted me concerning a parishioner who was worried about his dead wife because she had previously been married to a man who had also died. Now that she was dead, the parishioner believed she might be having a good time with her former husband. I had been so amused by the story that I hadn't taken it seriously. Yet that man's problem made about as much sense as my inclination to worry about whether or not my wife would remarry after my death. I determined to give the idea no more thought.

My second experience with death had come three years after my father's death when we again gathered in a bedroom, this time my mother's, and watched while her pain-filled body gave up its struggle and became quiet. She had been sick for two years and had suffered tremendously. The expense of her illness had been terrific, and it had been only through good fortune that my brother and I had been able to pay the bills. At least my own death would not leave my family so destitute. Her going had been a release: a release for her from pain and helplessness; a release for my brother from long hours of worry, of nursing care, and of hard work to meet medical bills; a release for us all from the anxiety, the tension, the impact of her cries upon us. We missed her terribly, but the illness had been so long. When it was over, we felt a certain relief.

I hoped my own illness would not have that effect when it was finished. Just how to prevent such a result would take some figuring, which I had better get at while my thinker was functioning clearly, but now I was tired from the memories that had claimed the morning. Now I needed to rest, to turn my mind into the quietness that had given me rest and peace and forgetting when I discovered yesterday what I was facing. I searched my mind for a scriptural passage by which I could enter the quietness.

> "Come unto me," a voice said,
> "Come unto me all ye that labor . . . and I
>   will give you rest" (Matt. 11:28, KJV).
> Rest and a forgetting;
> Rest and peace from labor;
> The labors of yesterday when my body
>   was strong.
> I come unto Thee, Quiet Person of the
>   shepherd fields:
> Quiet Figure that waits beside the still
>   waters of the spirit,

That walks with one in green pastures of
the soul,
To give one rest and peace.
The labors of the body He accepts,
And the burdens of the mind He lifts
from me,
And I am quiet.
I am the child and He the Parent;
I am the son and He the Father,
Out upon the road to welcome me as I
trudge homeward.
I was afraid, but now I am not;
I was tired, but now I am rested;
I was resentful, but now I am eager:
Eager and hopeful, anxious and joyful.
The days of yesterday fade away from me,
and the plans of tomorrow are gone;
The day of the new hope approaches;
The tasks of tomorrow arrive;
My hope and the hope of the saints lay
hold of me.
I come and Thou dost receive me.
Thy robe and Thy cloak do enfold me;
I rest from my labors, the hard tasks I
have known:
The fears and the follies are past;
The morrow is bright and faith strong
within me.
I rest: I thank Thee, God, for Thy peace.

3. Routine

Gradually, almost without my realizing it, my days fell into an orderly routine during the last weeks of my illness. A routine is a great boon to one who is going through something difficult, for it helps one avoid having to make decisions about little things that do not deserve full attention. It is like a ritual that does not need to be constantly questioned but can be trusted to achieve the objective it was devised to accomplish. Some people never seem to be able to create and follow a routine—and what miserable, disorderly, noncreative, irritating persons I think they are! They have difficulty knowing which shoe to put on first and which necktie to wear, what to have for breakfast, how to get to work, when to go home, and especially when to go to bed. Other people make their major decisions and set up the routine of their lives, but they have difficulty following it.

Another group of individuals can follow a routine if someone else works it out for them, but they would never devise one themselves, and they become panic-stricken if they have to vary from it in the least. These people always do just the right thing at the right time, wear just the right combinations of colors, and are always on time for every appointment. They never commit an unbecoming act and cannot understand why anyone else would ever do so. These are not the Judases who betray their Master, nor the Peters who deny Him; they have neither the imagination nor the doubtful courage that would lead to such actions. They are the Pilates who follow the whims of the crowd; or rather, they are the members of the crowd who cry out for a crucifixion once they have been directed to parrot such a cry. They are slaves to routine; often they are found doing a useful kind of task, which someone else has delegated to them and which someone else directs.

The routine I fell into during the closing days of my earthly life was like that. Someone else devised it to help me meet the encroaching pain and weakness. My routine started early in the morning, for I awoke somewhat earlier than the rest of the household. Until toward the very end (when I was dependent upon others for my total nursing care), I would get up, wash and shave, and return to bed. Presently there came breakfast and pleasant conversation, medicine, the morning news, bath, the fixing of room and bed, reading, writing, rest; lunch, rest, reading or writing again, callers, rest; supper, long visits and listening to music with my wife or a friend, and then bed again. The rest periods were characterized by quiet reading and meditation when I sought to free my spirit from the things about me and to practice what the medieval mystic Brother Lawrence called "the practice of the presence of God." During these periods I consciously attempted to give over the tensions that filled my body and soul, particularly the regrets and longings, in order that I might lay hold upon the Spirit of the universe. As time passed, this Presence became more and more real.

In a certain sense, that was the overarching problem of my death, rooted in my desire to die with dignity and ease. I had to accept God, who had been taken for granted and who had been real only in brief moments — I had to accept Him and let Him take possession of my entire self, of my hopes and plans and desires, both for myself and my loved ones. I had to recognize and accept the fact that the things I had looked forward to seeing accomplished by my students, friends, and children would go forward without me. Those had been my plans. I had outlined them, raised money for them, and otherwise provided for them. Those plans may still be carried through, but I will have no further vital part in them.

As the days passed I welcomed certain selected students; I actually sent for some whom I liked and whose future I was particularly concerned about. They came eagerly, but they lacked a certain spontaneity in my presence that they had possessed previously. I carried the major burden of the conversations. They followed my thoughts with dogged devotion, but most of them lacked the spark that makes for restfulness in human relationships, especially when one is ill and one's mental faculties are below par. These gradually stopped coming, for I did not encourage their calls. One or two students and several neighbors and colleagues were a definite burden and took a great deal out of me. After a short time I specifically asked that certain persons not be admitted to my room. In all but two or three instances, it was possible to protect me from such persons. It is unfortunate that some people are so insensitive, even in the face of death, that they do not know when they are being harmful, and they sometimes occupy positions in relation to one that make it impossible or embarrassing to tell them that they should not impose their presence, however well-intended, upon a sick person.

I learned that one may use certain defenses with varying degrees of success, depending upon how desperate you become, and depending on the position the offender holds in relation to you and your family. The first part of this defense consists of being noncommunicative, either in words or in smiles, which indicate the degree of response on your part. Again, the effectiveness of this strategy depends upon just how rough you wish to be upon the caller, as well as how protective of your own strength you feel you must be.

Second, upon a bothersome visitor's entrance to your room, you do not offer to shake hands, and you do not ask your caller to sit down. Of course, the visitor may do both of these things anyway, regardless of your failure to encourage it. If so, then it is entirely proper to open your entire arsenal of resistance, for such a person deserves whatever he may get.

Such a visitor comes to see you not because of a concern for you, but because that person's position dictates that he call. He considers this call a flattery to you, so he insists upon visiting you, regardless of what he does to you or you to him. When he asks you how you are feeling (as he inevitably will, despite the fact that such a question is almost certain to remind you of your approaching death), you should mumble that you feel "pretty good," but not overdo your response. After he has told you how busy he is and how difficult it is to find time to come to see you, grunt noncommittally or disinterestedly. If you overdo the disinterested attitude or show an inclination to disbelieve him, your caller will enter into an argument calculated to overcome your resistance, and all will be lost.

Do not ask questions, or the offensive visitor will answer them. It also is important to answer any that are asked you vaguely and in as uninterested a tone as possible. If two persons have come to call (as they often do because they are basically afraid of coming alone), you are apt to be subjected to unreasonable punishment, for one will feed the ego of the other so that they will be certain to stay too long. However, in that situation you have a less important role to play since they will largely ignore you.

After a time, my wife and I hit on a plan that never failed to work with either man or woman, for women are just as prone as men to overstay in their calls upon the sick. When such a visitor came, my wife would disappear, leaving the person in the room with me alone, since her presence only stimulated an even greater exhibition of pomposity. After a time I would clutch my stomach, hold my breath, and press my lips together tightly, looking toward the bathroom quite mysteriously. Then I would utter in a hushed tone of voice, "I wonder if you could call my *wife* . . . or perhaps you would. . . . No, maybe you had better call her." My visitor never failed to rush out looking for her, greatly relieved that I had not insisted he help me; and since it was understood between us that she was not to be nearby, the caller was frequently in a state of near panic by the time he found her. Upon only one visitor did we have to use the device more than once. With the others, after that, a bit of restlessness on my part was sufficient to send them on their way. Some never returned at all.

It was unfortunate that my friends did not have enough understanding when I was seriously ill to permit us to send them word when their calls would be most helpful, but such was not the case. My minister and my doctor were more sensitive in this regard, although both used to drop by occasionally on unscheduled calls. Both knew of their welcome, and both came for the sake of my wife as much as for mine. To both I said, "When I need you especially I will send for you, but come whenever you can, regardless."

It was toward the end that they were both most helpful; both contributed to my morale and from the poise of both I drew heavily: my doctor in a human sense and my minister in a more definitely spiritual sense, for he helped me increasingly to hold the reality of God in my mind even when the reality of other things slipped away from me. Increasingly, I strived to rest in Him whose desires were greater than my desire, whose hopes were beyond my hopes, whose understanding surpassed my understanding, and in whose affection my affection rested. I did this through reading some favorite selections of verse, prayers, or Scripture. Closing the book and lying back with my eyes closed, I permitted my mind to become saturated with the phrases, seeking to penetrate deeper into their *meaning.*

One that was quite meaningful to me was the prayer written by that great soul John Henry Newman:

> O Lord, support us all the day long of this
>   troublous life,
> Until the shadows lengthen and the
>   evening comes,
> And the busy world is hushed,
> And the fever of life is over,
> And our work is done.
> Then in Thy mercy
> Grant us a safe lodging,
> And a holy rest,
> And peace at the last.
> Through Jesus Christ our Lord. *Amen.*

Over and over again I prayed it, running certain of the phrases through my mind until my spirit was caught up and carried away in them:

> *O Lord, support us all the day long;*
> In the early morning, support us;

In the full-blown effort of midday,
Until the coming evening, support us.
Support us with Thy love and Thy
    affection,
Support us in heated moments,
And through pain-filled moments;

O Lord, support us until the evening comes —
The evening with its cool restfulness,
The evening with its growing quietness;
Help us to give over our busy coming
    and going
To give over the fever of life —
And accept the evening and the deep
    night.

A holy rest and peace at the last:
May Thy great mercy enfold us,
And give us rest,
The sure rest that comes from Thee;
Rest that claims us when we are free,
When our minds and spirits are free from
    life's hurried concerns.

Support us, O Lord —
Thou hast given us support;
Forgive us, O Lord —
Thou hast forgiven us;
We return to Thee, O Lord,
Our talents and our blessings;

We repent of the times they have been
    buried and hidden away,
Caught in the tensions of living;
Smothered in the confusion of busyness;
Forgive us, O Lord, for our preoccupations,
Our strong desires and willfulness;
The fever of life has laid hot hands upon us
And we have rushed hither and yon;
O Lord, forgive us.

Father out upon the road to meet us,
Robe and fatted calf await us,
We cannot believe it;
Lord, dost Thou now forgive us?
"In my father's house are many mansions"
    (John 14:2, KJV).
"Many mansions" Jesus spoke of,
Mansions of the soul to dwell in;
To rest in peace and dwell forever
In the mansions of the spirit,
In the mansions of the soul.
In Thy sure support we wait,
As the evening closes round us,
A holy rest creeps over us,
And enfolds us in Thy peace.

"In My Father's house are mansions,"
Mansions that are now before us;
O Lord, we are grateful,
For Thy mercy and Thy peace.

4. Reflection

One day I sat reflecting. Now that my illness was far advanced, my mind was filled with thoughts of the world beyond me. These thoughts were shared only with my wife and my minister, for others would be distressed by them. Perhaps my minister was distressed too, but he never revealed it in my presence, for he was a disciplined person and well prepared for the task of standing beside one who is soon to go on beyond the limits of earthly living. His quiet hope and pleasant manner were a balm and a benediction. Sometimes we said little but sat quietly together, each occupied with his own thoughts; then he would rise, say a brief prayer, and leave. Sometimes when I awoke I found him sitting quietly beside the window reading. Sometimes it was my wife or a neighbor friend. Curious how one does not like to be alone at such a time, probably because of the terror caused by the drugs and fever and confusion, and by the regrets openly expressed by those who come into one's room.

That day as I sat reflecting upon the "kingdom" I was soon to enter, I thought of a letter a missionary wrote to a friend: "I have just learned that I am soon to die. It may be that by the time you receive this I shall have gone on. Do not bother to answer; I will see you in the morning." There was a man of faith. *I will see you in the morning.*

A friend of mine who was on a ship that was torpedoed during World War II, and who spent ten days on a raft, said, "It's amazing how religious you can get under those conditions." A chaplain reported that after each enemy bombing raid, the attendance at his chapel services increased. It was so obvious that when the attendance dropped, the men would joke, "Chaplain, we need another raid."

We have often belittled this tendency to become religious in time of danger, yet it is deep in the hearts of all of us. The tendency is understandable, but I never thought it reasonable to believe that our prayers under such conditions would change what was happening to me. For that reason, I have not always prayed in the face of suffering and danger, "Thy will be done" (Matt. 6:10, KJV). Instead I have prayed, "O Lord, fill my spirit with Thy Spirit" (see Eph. 3:14–19).

May Thy Spirit come into my spirit and
    make it Thine own . . .
Spirit of God, high and lifted up,
God of the quiet places, God of the
    strong,
Fill my spirit with Thy Spirit.
I repent of heated moments that have
    claimed me.
I repent of hurried moments when I have
    forgotten Thee,
When tensions have laid hold upon me
    and have filled me.
Fill my spirit with Thy Spirit, God of the
    living, God of the dead.

Fill my spirit with Thy Spirit, God of the
    living, God of the dead;
God of the hopeful, God of the lonely.
My body is filled with pain, and my mind
    is burdened with terror:
These have crept over me; and have
    claimed me. . . .
They have torn at my poise and de-
    stroyed my sense of dignity.
Dark dreams have claimed me and
    doubts have possessed me.

Fill my spirit with Thy Spirit, God of the
    nations;
God of the sunset and God of the skies;

God of the suffering and God of the
laughter;
God of freedom and God of hope;
God of affection and God of love.

Fill my spirit with Thy Spirit that I may
live,
God of the prophets, and God of the
saints;
God of our Lord and God of the poets;
Fill my spirit with Thy Spirit,
And make me whole.
I rest in Thee . . . rest in peace and quiet-
ness;
I rest in Thee . . . in Thy peace and
quietness.
God of Jesus . . . Lord and Savior. *Amen.*

5. Understanding

The process of dying is a curious thing. Many times I had sat beside the beds of persons as the end approached and wondered how much a dying person knew of what goes on in the room. I suppose it varies a great deal, but with me I knew most of what was happening until the last thirty-six hours. After that, I was aware of some things, but much of it didn't interest me. Already my mind and spirit had moved on to other things even while my body struggled out its last hours, fighting on beyond all reason or sense. This struggle was out of my control, which made me feel like a bystander.

A woman friend of my wife's came in and wept quite openly and profusely. I was somewhat amused by her. She had no idea that I knew what was going on; even my nurse and my doctor thought I was in a deep coma. Her weeping was quite out of keeping with the attitude of all of us. Poor soul. She felt so badly, but I recognized—and I hoped the others would too—that she wept not because of what was happening to me, but because of some experience with death that had happened to her sometime in the past. I wanted to tell her to stop her weeping, but she might have been shocked, and I'm sure my wife would have thought me unkind.

I tried not to pay much attention to what happened during those last three or four days. It was hard, because various people kept thinking of things that would make me more comfortable. I would have been comfortable enough if they had only let me alone.

The dying experience happens to a person only once, so it is hard to do it well. As one fellow said about practicing jumping out of an airplane, "What's the use of practicing something you have to do perfectly the first time?"

As I became increasingly worse and was confined to my room, my interests shifted. I gave up reading the newspaper and listening to the radio except for selected music. My eyesight became poor, so I read only a little poetry and selected Bible verses. Often these were read to me by my minister or my wife. My interest was limited to the immediate room, to a part of the room, to those who came to my room, and finally to the voices that came out of the darkness beside me. During this later stage, I heard only what I wished to hear. It had been some time since I had taken any interest in world events, in politics, in social justice, and in affairs at the university. I was always a follower of sports, and my interest in them was one of the last things to go; but finally sports lost their capacity to hold me, and I found myself only vaguely concerned with the outcome of events that formerly had seemed so important. Fewer and fewer persons were admitted to my room as I recognized that they were often at a loss to know what to say. When I realized this, I asked that they be relieved of their sense of obligation to call.

I was still interested in music. I remembered a story that Richard C. Cabot, M.D., told about a dying patient in Boston who asked him to play his violin for her. He canceled his appointments, went to her home, and spent the afternoon playing quietly, selection after selection, in the adjacent room so that the movements of the artist would not tire the sick woman. When I heard of this incident, I realized that motion in a sick room can be tiring. That was my own experience later; any motion was tiring, and the movements of more than one person in the sickroom were very exhausting. Through the afternoon, Dr. Cabot had played as the woman slipped into a coma and on into death. The doctor counted that experience as one of the occasions when he knew his efforts had made a difference. He referred to it often years later.

Remembering Dr. Cabot's story, I asked that a phonograph be placed in the adjacent room where I could hear it, but where it could be tended without my bothering with it. This was done, and it played steadily and quietly those last days.

Even as I moved toward a deeper coma, I could hear and respond to certain words, especially, "Our Father which art in heaven . . . " (Matt. 6:9, KJV). *Our Father, my Father . . .* I had never been especially close to my father, but through the years I had learned that fatherhood and parenthood meant understanding and affection. It did not mean a strange land filled with strange and hostile people but friendly and loving people. This thought, vague and somewhat misty, reassured me. But it was hard to hold this thought in mind as the pain and fever mounted and as my mind became more and more confused under the impact of the increasing doses of drugs that Fred, my doctor, administered. He had given his promise that he would keep me comfortable, and he was keeping his word. But the drugs caused me to have nightmares. Maybe it wasn't the drugs that caused it; maybe they only permitted it. Anyway, I had some wild ones. I told Fred about it, and he changed the drug; after that it was better, especially as I began to draw more heavily on the words of life. I would relax my body as completely as I could and then let the words flow through my mind, slowly, peacefully, quietly:

Our Father which art in heaven,
    In heaven and in earth,
    Beyond the earth and within the earth;
Thou who hast created the earth and
Given it the spark of life.
    God of the earth and God of the heavens,
Of life and death, of birth and of growth.
These I have thought upon;
    And then I heard the little man
Who views life with the skeptic's eye,
    Who proudly squares his shoulders
    and looks into the sky,
And with a giant's stance, shouts to the
    elements,
"There is no god, nor orderliness,
No heaven, nor immortality;
    Blind happenstance rides the earth and
    sky, and hurls the human creature
    Through his little crises and his hopes;
His longings and his faith a foolishness,
His courage and his heroism,
An empty echo that falls on empty ears."

The skeptic's voice has often been a
    prayer,

His crying out a hope, an uttered hope,
That God would hear and strike him
   dumb
To still his voice of doubt,
And fill his mind and soul with certain
   knowledge;
His doubting mind wants little doubt,
His stumbling hope seeks certain hope;
Yet he, for all his mental powers,
Admits no faith unexplored,
No courage that moves forward
Into the darkness of untread paths.
The skeptic cannot lead the way—
He only lifts a sound.
A baying buoy in the sea,
A ringing bell that warns the passer-
   by.
He never has the privilege of sailing in or
   out,
But through the storms and through the
   tides,
He waits and sounds his haunting cry,
To those who pass him by.

I have often thought—
It seems quite reasonable—
That God and heaven do exist
Only for those who think the thought;
Who live and move and fill their minds
With hope instead of doubt;

Who face into the future with courage
    strong.
Their faith becomes a highway,
And their confidence the guide,
To find undreamed-of vistas of the soul
That stretch into the future's endless way,
To immortality, that throbs with zestful
    laughter
And with tears; with life
As we know it here, so there;
Life that is filled as our lives are filled
With joys and sadness and creative tasks.
To have laughter without tears,
Joy without the longing and the doubt,
Would be to have an empty heaven,
One without the zest of heaven here;
    To have a gift too easy and too filled
    with emptiness.

Our Father, we worship Thee,
Holy be Thy name;
Thy Kingdom come, Thy will be done
On earth as it is in heaven;
Thy will be done. . . .

Thy will has not been done — we have not
    known it;
Thy will has not been done — when we
    have known it;
Thou hast a will for us, we have believed:

Thou hast created us and made us strong,
Thou hast created us and given us a will
  of our own.
Strong wishes within us and strong
  desires
Often lay hold upon us and drive us on;
Wills clash and worlds clash,
Ours and Thine own;
Storms lash across the good earth,
Destroying and tearing that which Thou
  created,
A part of Thine own.
Is this war within the Godhead?
Is this strife within Thyself?
If there is such grim destruction
Going on within creation,
Then the clash of wills within us,
Clash of strong desires inside us,
Is a part of heaven's longing
And is part of heaven's hope.
The skeptic's doubt and loud shouting
Are within each person's soul,
Sounding out his shouts and warnings
To each passing thought and effort.
Some are caught and cannot pass by,
Others nod and trudge on strongly,
Warned, they move on homeward,
Knowing that the bell buoy is but an
  echo,
Flickering out its light and sound,

But beyond and further onward
Is the true and stronger purpose,
Is the purpose and true meaning
Of the suffering and the longing,
Of the hope and constant yearning
Of the pulling of the soul.

So I prayed and so I brooded
In the days of yesteryear;
Now all that is passed
And I pray the larger prayer—
Thine the kingdom, glory, Father,
Thine the power, the heaven home.
So be it, Lord and Father;
So be it, God and Friend,
Amen and amen.

6. Further Thoughts

Last night I died. Today has been rather restful. There has been a lot of coming and going today around the house, but I haven't been bothered by it. This business of dying is often so long and drawn out that everybody is exhausted when it is over. Maybe that's just as well, because the awareness of what is happening is not so acute. It seems to be harder on youngsters than anyone else. They just can't understand what is happening.

I must confess I was pretty worn out myself, although Fred did do a good job according to his understanding of the way I was feeling. The sicker I got, the less I cared about the things those around me were concerned about. A few of our friends made a great to-do. Fortunately, my wife and I had foreseen some of this in our discussions. My wife didn't think God was killing me, and she wasn't impressed by some of the senti-mental talk about my going.

I no longer think about the things I left un-done. I remember a medical intern named Dick Morris who said, "When I die and go to that place where doctors go and sit down around the table with the great and near-great, I hope I'll be able to say, 'I hurt no person I treated; I took no other doctor's patient; I helped a few people.'" That's the kind of contentment I found as I looked back across my life these last few weeks.

Today it's a relief not to have to bother with a bath when it hurts so much to be moved, or with eating when I don't feel up to it. It seems odd to shift all of a sudden from one world to another where things that were so very important yes-terday aren't important at all now.

They took my body to the funeral parlor and got it all fixed up in a handsome casket, with flow-ers arranged around it. People are coming to look at it and some of them are saying, "My! Doesn't he look nice?" I never thought a fellow's body would look better dead than alive, but it must be so, judging by the things people are saying.

I hope my wife remembers not to be too sad at the funeral, especially at the grave. It's a me-morial service, and I hope she remembers that they are not burying "me" — not the eternal I. None of that, "Look at your father. It's the last time you'll ever see him" nonsense such as my aunt pulled on me at my father's death. It took me years to get over that, and even now the memory of it gives me the willies! Of course, it's all right to bury my body. They have to do something with it, and I suppose it should be treated with dignity.

It seems odd that a lot of people avoid thinking about these things before they actually die. They prefer not to know they are dying, so they don't talk with their wives or husbands about things they could solve simply by being realistic. I don't mean that a person has to be morbid. I believe that talking about death simply means that one is thoughtful and considerate of others. Many people never even inquire how they are getting along during an illness, preferring not to know if they are facing death. They gradually become worse, sink into unconsciousness, and die without having turned their minds into the quietness to link their thoughts with God. There is a dignity to life and a dignity to death. Why deprive yourself of that?

Oh, there's the benediction. Apparently, I missed my own funeral! I often heard people joke about that, but never expected it to happen to me.

I've got to be going. I'll be seeing you around one of these days.

Part II

Christian Reflections on Death

7. The Contemplation of Death Enriches Life

Thomas S. Kepler

We are faced with but two certainties amidst all our various experiences. First, we know that we are alive. Each of us can say, "I am." In making this affirmation, we are aware of the mystery of life: that we came into existence as human beings, that our minds and bodies are curiously interrelated, that we can achieve purpose and adventure in the years that are ours, that we can have a personal relationship with God, and that we are challenged to live with other human beings who are quite different from ourselves. To be *alive* is one of life's certainties. Second, we know that we will die someday. No one escapes the mystery of death!

As human beings have had different philosophies of life, they also have possessed various attitudes toward death. Some have feared it; others have welcomed it. I remember my conversation not long ago with a person in his late eighties, a man who had lived courageously and unselfishly through the years. He said to me: "I can hardly wait until I meet death. My physical body is no longer strong and in many ways is a burden to me. I am looking forward to the experience we call 'death,' for I shall then be released from the burden of this old physical body and shall be able to enjoy the new experiences which lie ahead of me when my spirit is clothed in its new 'glorified' body!" His view of death was full of faith. It spoke deeply to my own experience.

Each of us should take time to think seriously about our own death. Years ago I set aside a period of time to express my own philosophy of death. I called it, "The Contemplation of Death Enriches Life."[1]

It is winter, 1945. I am sitting in my office, thinking about death—particularly *my* death. It brings me no sense of morbidity to realize that my span of life on this planet will probably terminate in twenty-five years or so.[2] Rather, it gives to me a drive to do the

---

[1]Thomas S. Kepler, *Credo: Fundamental Christian Beliefs* (Nashville, Tenn.: Abingdon-Cokesbury Press, 1945), 78–89.

[2]Editor's Note: Dr. Kepler died twenty-two years after this was written.

worthwhile things I want done . . . an incentive to be more kind and helpful to the people I meet . . . an impetus to live *this day* as though it were the last and best day of my existence.

Outside it is snowing. The snowflakes are falling patiently and kindly, lodging securely on the boughs of the campus trees. Through the soft snow curtain, I discern the spire of the college chapel pointing upward as though to direct my thoughts to God. The sight of the chapel reminds me of the 1,600 students who have walked in and out of its doors, now on the fighting fronts of the world. I realize that death is imminent to many of them. I try to parallel their thoughts of death with mine. I conclude that many of them are weighing death in possible terms of moments, while I am weighing my death in terms of years. That is the difference. I want to live my life as courageously and dynamically in the years ahead as they are forced to live under the expediency of war in these tragic days. The thought of death deepens my desire to live!

I arise from my chair and say to myself, "I am not afraid of death. I believe that death is necessary in order to enrich life."

1. Death is a part of the totality of our experience; it is never something separate from life. It is synonymous with selfless living. Said Jesus, "Those who lose their life for my sake will find it" (Matt. 10:39b). This dictum describes the Christian's experience in this temporal span of experience; it is not merely an insight into that moment when every person adventurously steps from a space-time world into the realm of the eternal. In daily living, the Christian learns how to die. Said the apostle Paul, "I die every day!" (1 Cor. 15:31).

There is a bundle of selfless desires within each person. If it is the native purpose of a child to be selfish, it is the sacred task of a maturing person to die daily to egocentricity. However, one can graduate even from human altruism to be resurrected to a higher kind of living.

Two contemporary writers well describe the shift that must be made if one is to learn the art of dying in order to obtain worthwhile living. One writer describes a woman called Edith who was "a little country bounded on the north, south, east, and west — by Edith." Edith never had graduated from childish egocentricity. The other novelist has one of her characters say, "Life's just too much trouble unless one can live for something big!" This dying from the Edith-type of self and living to the type of selflessness patterned by the girl who would "live for something big" is at the heart of Christian experience. To "die every day" to selfish living is necessary if life is to be lived according to the Christian pattern; it is the avenue to the resurrected life of unselfish love.

Voltaire poignantly illustrates what I mean. In his earlier years, before he had established a constructive viewpoint of life, he said, "I hate to live, and yet I am afraid to die." In the last days of his life, he remarked, "I die now, loving my friends, not hating my enemies, adoring God and detesting superstition." Fear of death had shifted in his experience so that the thought of death enriched his life. Like the spirit of the apostle Paul, beautifully framed in the words of Robert Southwell, Voltaire had learned, "Not where I breathe, but where I love, I live." The proper thought of death causes one to die to pride, suspicion, resentment, fear, jealousy; it resurrects one to a life imbued with love. The person who learns how to "die every day" will find it but natural to meet death with a faith akin to George Matheson's:

> O Love that wilt not let me go,
>   I rest my weary soul in Thee;
> I give Thee back the life I owe,
>   That in Thine ocean depths its flow
> May richer, fuller be.

2. *We have a rendezvous with death; we also have a rendezvous with life. The thought of death intensifies our urge to live.* The tragic circumstances of war deepen our thinking about both life and death. Among the poets who sang their phrases about death in World War I, none spoke a higher word than Alan Seeger:

> I have a rendezvous with Death,
> At some disputed barricade,
> When Spring comes back with rustling
>   shade
> And apple blossoms fill the air—
> I have a rendezvous with Death
> When Spring brings back blue days and
>   fair.

While this was a poem for war, it also expresses every human being's feeling about death in time of peace. Like Alan Seeger, who laid down his pen and kept his rendezvous, so must every one of us keep a tryst with death. War only emphasizes the immediacy of death. Peacetime is more patient in bringing this experience to most of us. Yet both war and peace challenge us not merely to die but also to live with intensity.

Alan Seeger's graphic words were mirrored by Countee Cullen, then an eighteen-year-old African-American boy and a senior in a New York City high school, who spoke about his rendezvous with life:

> I have a rendezvous with Life,
> In days I hope will come,
> Ere youth has sped, and strength of mind,
> Ere voices sweet grow dumb.
> I have a rendezvous with Life,
> When Spring's first heralds hum.

Proper thought of death should be constructive; it should urge a person to live with every degree of intensity. It should make one want to spend each moment richly, in order to feel heroism and adventure as a part of life's total experience. A friend of mine expresses this attitude toward life thus:

> Afraid to live? Nay, I would grow,
> Triumph, conquer, fail, forego.

On the tomb of a minister buried a few blocks from my study, I recently saw this inscription:

> I preached as never sure to preach again,
> And as a dying man to dying men.

When I asked one of my friends about this minister (a person who had known him well), he said, "Yes, that inscription well describes him. He died in 1886 at the age of twenty-eight years. On his pulpit he kept that quotation; it was the motivation for his living as well as his preaching. He lived every moment with great intensity, as though it might be the last—and also the best—moment of his life."

The creative thought of death drives a person to consider every hour of life experience as a giant hour. Because we have been given by God the privilege of living, we do not wish to waste such an experience. We want it to count for something. We want to live with a sense of purposeful immediacy.

Wise physicians do not conceal the incurability of a disease from a patient; they know that the knowledge of death aids the patient and the patient's family to plan with wisdom the time remaining. This was the case with Grant Wood, the artist, who in going to the hospital consented to an examination only if the doctors would tell him what malady they might find. The doctors kept their promise; they told him that he had an incurable cancer. When he was informed of this malignancy, he resigned from the staff of the University of Iowa because he knew he would never leave the hospital bed. The university refused his resignation—one of the most warming experiences he ever had. Until the end Grant Wood courageously and creatively lived in his hospital room: the thought of death intensified the living of his remaining days.

No more inspiring story has come out of World War II than the one of the four chaplains who served on the *Dorchester,* a United States transport ship sunk in February 1943 by a submarine off the coast of Greenland. The chaplains gave their life preservers to four of the combatant men on the boat who were without preservers, since as chaplains they had promised to care for their men in every need. Last reports of these four chaplains—George Fox and Clark Poling, Protestant ministers; Alexander Goode, a Jewish rabbi; and John Washington, a Roman Catholic priest—portrayed them on the sinking ship, arms about one another, singing, "Nearer, My God, to Thee"! If, in the last few moments before a rendezvous with death, human beings can have such an intensified, courageous rendezvous with life, ought it not to be possible that the whole span of life be lived with a similar intensity? The thought of death does intensify the urge to live if death is seen in its proper perspective.

8. The Little Deaths

Douglas V. Steere

Death is usually thought to be one experience that precedes the grave, but it is more than that. Death is a continuous experience in which a person dies "little deaths" each day. In dying these "little deaths" daily, one is also being resurrected daily to a higher type of spiritual selfhood. Hence, the apostle Paul wrote to the Roman Christians: "For if we have been united with [Christ] in a death like his, we will certainly be united with him in a resurrection like his. . . . If we have died with Christ, we believe that we will also live with him" (Rom. 6:5, 8). In one of his last letters, to the Philippians, Paul saw that he was still dying to his lower self and emerging toward a Christlike character: "I press on toward the goal for the prize of the heavenly call of God in Christ Jesus" (Phil. 3:14).

One of the most beautiful books on the devotional life is written by Douglas V. Steere, Quaker philosopher of Haverford College. Its title is *On Beginning from Within*, and it contains a chapter entitled, "Death's Illumination of Life," given in April 1942 as the Ingersoll lecture on immortality at Harvard University.[1] From that lecture we have excerpted the meditation, "Practice in Dying: The Little Deaths." With both beauty and depth, this meditation shows dying as an experience encountered by every person each day.

These memories of the times when we took what John Donne calls the "Northerne Passage," when we risked, when we practiced dying by dying the little deaths only to have something come alive within us, are not conclusive evidence of immortality. They are at best only hints and intimations, but they seem to have prepared us for change and individuation, and so at death they are good company.

How good to remember, now, that time in life when as a parent we saw a child off to school that first morning, to feel the wrench of his departure, to know that now he must make his own way, be taught by others than ourselves, risk life

---

[1] Douglas V. Steere, *On Beginning from Within* (New York: Harper & Brothers, 1943), 132–135.

by accidents and suffer in countless ways from which we can no longer shield him! We trusted him to life that morning, and as he disappeared from sight, we died a little death. But in that death something still stronger inside us seemed to emerge, and he was more our own because we had let him go.

How good to remember the first day we gave a daughter in marriage to a young man who was not bone of our bone and who could scarcely be expected to understand and to treat this precious daughter as we knew so well to do at home! How great the risks and uncertainties of love and marriage! How important this girl's future was to our heart! And then the scene cleared, and we gave her away to this young man. And we died another little death, only to feel a new dimension of caring for these two rise up in us and the meaning of an old Sanskrit proverb come clear: "That which is not given away is lost."

How good in this hour to remember the day when our mother or our father died! It seemed as if they must always be there, that they must always come to us in illness or distress, that they could always be relied upon. Any tasks well done, there was a secret sense of their approval; any recognition our work received, it was the prospect of their satisfaction in that acknowledgment that made up the greater share of any worth that it possessed. Then perhaps the mother died, and there came a rush of mingled loss and of being cut adrift. Now you were alone at sea. Now you must steer your course alone. Now you were adult. Now you bore the full responsibility.

Rainer Maria Rilke describes in the *Journal of My Other Self* how the physician fulfilled his father's wish at death and pierced the father's heart. At that moment the aloneness seemed complete, and he spoke to himself, "Today, Brigge, and nevermore." He describes the walk he took on that day about the town of his boyhood. Now it seemed a town for grown-up people. On this day the child in him had died the little death. But the *Me* in him knew a new depth to its love for and relationship with the father, and yet this *Me* knew its own root as never before.

How good to remember the time when I knew I should die if I owned to another my guilt in some affair, and how I owned it and died, only to discover that what had died in me in that miniature death was my egotistical pride, and that beneath the death of humiliation there is still the true *Me* that lives and breathes more freely for this loosening of its bonds!

How good to remember those sleepless nights when I feared to relax to sleep lest I should meet there what I was afraid of, and lest I should not be able to stand the encounter; and to remember how I slowly discovered that to die the little death of sleep meant trusting the goodness and the forgiving character of the conserver of the *Me,* and how I learned to let go to the source of life as the earth lets go to the spring, and how I was carried away and refreshed and strengthened and restored!

How good to remember that illness in which, my body stale, torpid, dull, and apathetic to my demands upon it, I practiced dying, I practiced wearing my body like a loose garment! There I discovered that instead of quenching the *Me,* the utter weakness of my body seemed to intensify the *Me's* claims to possess a life of its own.

How good to remember how I have let go what went before and have faced and welcomed each age of my life as it came, and in mature age how I have discovered that the dying back of my body has given me more occasion to be at home, and to keep my own heart warm by living in it! Until that time I had never fully grasped what that seventeenth-century writer meant when he suggested it was a wonderful thing to recognize the advanced age of a person less by the infirmity of his body than by the maturity of his soul.

And, finally, how good to remember how in prayer one day my stiff, tight, detailed petitions were all blown aside as though they were dandelion fluff, how I stopped praying and began to be prayed in, of how I died and was literally melted down by the love of a Power that coursed through my heart, sweeping away the hard claimful core, and poured through me a torrent of infinite tenderness and caring! Blind with tears, I suddenly knew and felt the very being of suffering people whom I had recently visited, gathered, and loved in the very heart of God, who drew me to care for them as I had never done in my days among them. Theresa of Avila once wrote of this death in prayer: "Nothing seemed to satisfy my desires; every moment my heart was ready to burst. It seemed to me as if my soul was being torn from me. It was a kind of death so delightful that my soul would gladly have prolonged it forever."

The remembrance of these exercises in dying the little deaths helps to make us able to inhabit a *Me* whose nature it seems to be to die into life, to discover an invisible means of support as it is loosened from its tightly clutched settings that masquerade as life.

9. Are We Immortal?

Winifred Kirkland

The Gospel of John ranks as great devotional literature, in which the resurrected Lord reigns in the life of the Christian believer. In this gospel the theme is, *Eternal life comes to the person who believes in Jesus Christ.* Eternal life in the Gospel of John, however, is not something one inherits at death; it is an experience of the risen Christ that begins now for the believer, this side of the grave. It continues also beyond the grave into eternity, where in our Father's house there are many rooms for all of us.

Winifred Kirkland, in her small book, *Are We Immortal?*,[1] shares the view of the Gospel of John: Immortality is something a Christian dares to live

---

[1] Winifred Kirkland, *Are We Immortal?* (New York: The Macmillan Company, 1941), 38–43.

now. As she writes this book during the evening years of her life, she ventures with Christian faith that God's plan will care for us throughout eternity. While this statement of faith cannot be proved by science, the rational person can make such an inference from what has been seen of earthly life. Eternal life, however, is not something to wait for; rather, it is something to begin living *here* and *now*.

And now after the rigors of a climbing lifetime I face the sunset. The evening radiance is becoming a beautiful and ever-increasing light. Presently that sun will dip to blackness for a moment, but only for a moment; then I shall feel myself walking unfettered, straight and free. And I think I shall find that all I had guessed is true. For this has been the guess on which I have built my philosophy, that the God of star and sea and flower is not mocked, least of all does He mock himself. In His creation, all the way from the first stir of life in water scum, . . . the ceaseless upward push of evolution is everywhere revealed. The urge is always toward personality, more and more highly perfected. Would a Creator suddenly toss to nothingness all the ultimate purpose of perfection, the individual human soul?

. . . Too long the whole concept of immortality has suffered from a most peculiar and lingering misconception, namely, that immortality is a state of being that occurs when we die! But if we are immortal at all, we are immortal now, this very moment. Why postpone our adjustment to a sublime condition? Let us be as fearlessly pragmatic in the discipline of our souls as of our bodies. It is amazing how completely tangled nerves relax, how simply anxieties are lifted, how a thousand fears evaporate, if once we incorporate into our daily philosophy of life the slogan, "Use your immortality now." Don't let us postpone the matching of our step to that of a Man who always walked immortally.

. . . It sometimes seems as if the real reason so many people resent the possibility of survival, of an endless ascending pilgrimage, is because immortality is a terrible responsibility to face. Negation is much easier to accept. For the Christian there is only one way to inure oneself to the inexorable splendor awaiting us, and that is to recognize each moment the companionship of a Man who achieved the impossible, to imitate each moment the daily conduct of the one Man of our climbing race who succeeded in living every day of His mortal life as if He were to live forever.

10. Heavenly Contemplation

Richard Baxter

Richard Baxter was one of the saintly figures of seventeenth-century England. Though ordained in the Church of England, he held great sympathy for the Puritans. In his later years he was imprisoned for his religious and political views. His classic volume, *The Saint's Everlasting Rest,* was written during a period of severe illness in Baxter's life. Its thoughts are clothed in a beautiful and robust language.

"The Nature of Heavenly Contemplation," from *The Saint's Everlasting Rest,* looks upon proper thoughts about eternal life or heaven as way to joyful preparation for the journey that lies ahead. Proper thoughts about death should bring one joy, comfort, and hope amidst the hardships of the present world.

This meditation is upon *your everlasting rest.* I would not have you cast off your other meditations; but surely, heaven should have preeminence in our meditation. That which will make us most happy when we possess it will make us most joyful when we meditate upon it. Other meditations are as numerous as there are lines in the Scripture or creatures in the universe, but the meditation upon heaven is a walk to Mount Zion—from the kingdoms of this world to the kingdom of saints, from earth to heaven, from time to eternity. Thoughts of your eternal destiny are like walking upon sun, moon, and stars in the garden and paradise of God.

You need not fear, like the men of the world, lest these thoughts should make you mad. It is in heaven and not hell that I persuade you to walk. It is joy and not sorrow that I persuade you to exercise. I urge you to look on no deformed objects, but only upon the ravishing glory of saints, the unspeakable excellencies of the God of glory, and the beams that stream from the face of His Son. Will it distract you to think of your only happiness? Will it distract the miserable to think of mercy, or the prisoner to foresee deliverance, or the poor to think of approaching riches and honor? I believe it should rather make someone mad to think of living in a world of woe, abiding in poverty and sickness among the rage of wicked people, than to think of living with

Christ in bliss. "Yet wisdom is vindicated by her deeds" (Matt. 11:19b). Knowledge has no enemy but the ignorant. This heavenly course of meditation is criticized only by those who never knew it or never used it. I fear more the neglect of this truth than anyone's opposition or arguments against it.

. . . A fitting time for such meditation is when you are in a suffering, distressed, or tempted state. When should we take refreshment but in time of fainting? When is it more timely to walk to heaven than when we know not in what corner of earth to live with comfort? Or when should we ponder things above more than when we have nothing but grief below? Where should Noah's dove be but in the ark when the waters cover all the earth and she cannot find rest for the sole of her foot? What should we think on but our Father's house when we have not even the husks of the world to feed upon? Surely God sends your afflictions for this very purpose. Happy are you if you make this use of your poverty! and you, sufferer, if you so spend your time of suffering! It is time to go to the promised land when our burdens are increased in Egypt!

Reader, if you knew what comfort in sorrow the serious views of your eternal glory can be, you would less fear these harmless troubles and more use that reviving remedy. "When the cares of my heart are many," David said to the Lord, "your consolations cheer my soul" (Ps. 94:19). The apostle Paul said, "I consider that the sufferings of this present time are not worth comparing with the glory about to be revealed to us" (Rom. 8:18). "So we do not lose heart. Even though our outer nature is wasting away, our inner nature is being renewed day by day. For this slight momentary affliction is preparing us for an eternal weight of glory beyond all measure, because we look not at what can be seen but at what cannot be seen; for what can be seen is temporary, but what cannot be seen is eternal" (2 Cor. 4:16–18).

Another time particularly fitting for this heavenly duty is when the messengers of God summon us to *die*. When should we more frequently sweeten our souls with the believing thoughts of another life than when we find that this is almost ended? No people have greater need of supporting joys than *dying* people; and these joys must be drawn from our eternal joy. As heavenly delights are sweetest when nothing earthly is mixed with them, so the delights of dying Christians are oftentimes the sweetest they ever had.

What a prophetic blessing had dying Isaac and Jacob for their sons! With what a heavenly song and divine benediction did Moses conclude his life! What heavenly advice and prayer had the disciples from their Lord when He was about to leave them! When Paul was ready to be "poured out like a drink offering" (2 Tim. 4:6, NIV), what heavenly exhortation and advice did he give the Philippians, Timothy, and the elders of Ephesus! How near to heaven was John in Patmos just before he died! It is the general temper of saints to be then most heavenly when they are nearest heaven. If it be your case, reader, to perceive your *dying* time is near, where should your heart now be but with Christ? I think you should even behold Him standing by you. You should speak to Him as your Father, your Husband, your Physician, your Friend. I think you should imagine the angels gathered around you, waiting to perform their last office to your soul—the angels that disdained not to carry Lazarus's soul into Abraham's bosom, nor will they hesitate to carry you there.

Look upon your pain and sickness as Jacob looked on Joseph's chariots (Gen. 45:21–28). Let your spirit revive within you to say, "It is enough. Christ is yet alive. Because He lives, I shall live also."

Do you need the choicest sweets to revive you? Here are better refreshments than the world can afford; here are all the joys of heaven, even the vision of God and Christ, and whatsoever the blessed will possess. These dainties are offered you by the hand of Christ. He has written the receipt in the promises of the gospel; He has prepared the ingredients in heaven. Only put forth the hand of faith to feed upon them, rejoice, and live.

The Lord says to you, as to Elijah, "Get up and eat, otherwise the journey will be too much for you" (1 Kings 19:7). Though it be not long, the way is miry; therefore obey His voice, arise and eat, and in the strength of this food you may go to the mount of God. Like Moses, "You shall die there on the mountain that you ascend" (Deut. 32:50) and say, as Simeon, "Master, now you are dismissing your servant in peace, according to your word; for my eyes have seen your salvation" (Luke 2:29–30).

11. On Death

Francis de Sales

One of the most beautiful and penetrating of the devotional classics is *Introduction to the Devout Life* by Francis de Sales. This volume, first published in 1608, is a layperson's primer for the devotional life. Though bishop of Geneva, Francis thought of himself primarily as a "director of souls." He looked upon worship as if it were a garden of flowers, which the worshiper leaves with a "spiritual nosegay" that will be a constant reminder of the beauty and majesty of God.

The Devout Life gives sane advice on all problems of religion, including the way a person meets death. Francis de Sales looked upon death as a journey. As a person takes pains to prepare for a regular journey, Francis believed he should make careful preparation for the journey of death.

PREPARATION

1. Place yourself in the presence of God.

2. Beseech Him to inspire you by His grace.

3. Imagine yourself to be in the extremity of sickness, lying on your deathbed, without any hope of recovery.

CONSIDERATIONS

1. Consider the uncertainty of the day of your death. *O my soul! You shall one day depart out of this body, but when shall the time be? Shall it be in winter or in summer? In the city or in the country? By day or by night? Shall it be suddenly or after due preparation? By sickness or by accident? Shall I have time to make my confession? Shall I be assisted by my spiritual director?* Alas! of all this we know nothing. One thing only is certain: We shall die, and sooner than we imagine.

2. Consider that then the world shall end for you, for it shall last no longer to you. It shall be reversed before your eyes. Then the pleasures, the vanities, the worldly joys, and vain affections of your life shall seem like empty shadows and airy clouds. *Ah, wretch! For what toys and deceitful vanities have I offended my God!* You shall then see that for a mere nothing you have forsaken Him. On the other hand, devotion and good works will then seem to you sweet and delightful. *Oh, why did I not follow this lovely and pleasant path?* Then the sins which before seemed very small will

appear as large as mountains and your devotion very small.

3. Consider the long and languishing farewell your soul shall then give to this poor world. She shall then bid adieu to riches, vanities, and vain company; to pleasures, pastimes, friends, and neighbors; to kindred, children, husband or wife. In a word, your soul shall take leave of every creature; *and* finally of her own body, which she shall leave pale, ghastly, hideous, and loathsome.

4. Consider how precipitously your neighbors will carry off your body to bury it under the earth, after which the world will think no more of you than you have thought of others. "The peace of God be with him," they shall say, and that is all. O death! How void you are of personal regard or pity!

5. Consider how your soul, being departed from the body, takes her flight to the right hand or to the left of God. Alas! Where shall yours go? What way shall it take? It pursues no other course than that which it began here in this world.

AFFECTIONS AND RESOLUTIONS

1. Pray to God, and cast yourself into His arms. *Ah! Receive me, O Lord, into Thy protection at that dreadful day! Make that hour happy and favorable to me, though all the other days of my life be sad and sorrowful.*

2. Despise the world. *Since then I know not the hour in which I must leave you, O wretched world, I will no more set my heart on you. O my dear friends and relations, pardon me if I love you no more but with a holy friendship, which may last eternally. For why should I unite myself to you, since I shall be one day forced to break those ties asunder?*

I will then prepare myself for that hour, and take all possible care to end this journey happily. I will secure the state of my conscience to the best of my power, and will form immediate and efficacious resolutions for the amendment of my defects.

CONCLUSION

Give thanks to God for these resolutions, which He has given you. Offer them to His Divine Majesty. Humbly ask Him to grant you a happy death, through the merits of the death of His beloved Son.

12. Remedies against Fear of Death

Jeremy Taylor

Recently speaking at an ecumenical meeting in an Ohio city, I was confronted by a man at the door after the service. He said to me, "I am terribly afraid of death!" What this man said probably expresses the feelings of many people. Death is a mystery, and what lies beyond the grave remains an enigma that only faith can attempt to fathom. However, most people who are afraid to die are also afraid to live. The basis for their fears is related to their lack of an abiding religious faith: In their self-centeredness, they distrust self rather than trust God.

Søren Kierkegaard, a profound Danish philosopher, once said, "There comes a midnight hour when all men must unmask." One of England's great bishops in the seventeenth century was Jeremy Taylor. He wrote two great classics, *Holy Living* and *Holy Dying.* In *Holy Dying*, he shows how we may prepare ourselves to face this "midnight hour when all men must unmask." He especially lays down ways by which the fear of death may be eliminated. He possesses remarkable insights into human nature and an understanding of the principles by which a person may replace fear of death with Christian courage, which will bring the believer a confidence of victory over death. "Remedies against Fear of Death" is from that volume.

1. Anyone who would be fearless of death must learn to despise the world. One must neither love any earthly thing passionately nor be proud of any circumstance in this life. "O death, how bitter is the thought of you to a man who is satisfied with his possessions, who has nothing to vex him, and who has great prosperity. Yes, you are despised even by him that is yet able to receive meat!" said the son of Sirach. On the other hand, a person who is not absorbed in passions for the things of this world will less fear to be divorced from them by a supervening death. Because one must part with them all in death, it is reasonable that one should not be passionate for such fleeting temporal interests. A woman may think herself a beautiful person or a man may fancy himself stronger and wiser than his neighbors. Each of them must remember that what they boast of will decline into weakness and dishonor. Then that very boasting and complacency will make death keener and more unwelcome, because it robs our earthly confidences and pleasures. Death makes our beauty equal to that of ladies who have slept some years in charnel houses, and our strength like the breath of an infant, and our wisdom like myths in a land where all things are forgotten.

2. *Anyone who would not fear death must have Christian fortitude.* This is more than human courage. To bear grief honestly and temperately, and to die willingly and nobly, is the duty of any good and valiant person. Those who do not so are commonly condemned as being vicious, and fools, and cowards. Everyone praises the valiant and honest among them.

The very heathen admire their heroes as examples of patience and bravery in the face of death. Zeno Eleates endured torments rather than betray his friends to the danger of a tyrant. Calanus of India willingly suffered himself to be burnt alive. All the Hindu women did so, to honor their husbands' memories and to prove their affections for their lords.

Yet Christianity commands more fortitude than any heathen institution ever did. We are commanded to be willing to die for Christ, to die for the brethren, to die alone rather than to give offense or scandal. The result? Anyone who does a Christian's duty is by the same instrument fortified against death. A Christian's duty is a Christian's security. It is certainly a great debasement of the gospel to regard death as something terrible to be avoided at all costs.

3. *Anyone who would not fear death must act courageously despite fear.* Fear gives to death wings, and spurs, and darts. Death hastens to a fearful man: If therefore you would make death harmless and slow, you must be heedless of your fears; and prayer is the way to do that. Cure your fear by a reflex act of prudence and consideration. They that fly from a battle are exposed to the fury of their pursuers who, if they faced about, were as well disposed to flee. At worst the losers can but die nobly; but now even at the very best they live shamefully or die timorously. Courage is the greatest security; for it often safeguards us but always rescues us from intolerable evil.

4. *If you would be fearless of death, anticipate conversing with the saints and angels.* Remember that there is a condition of living better than this; that there are creatures more noble than we; that above us there is a country better than ours; that the inhabitants of that country know more and know better and are in places of rest and desire. First learn to value their fellowship, then learn to purchase it, and death cannot be a formidable thing. The heathen believed it would be wonderful to pass from conversing with dull, ig-

norant, and foolish persons—with tyrants and enemies of learning—to meet Homer, Plato, Socrates, Cicero, Plutarch, and Fabricius in the afterlife. But we consider ours a higher privilege. Those who "die in the Lord" (Rev. 14:13) shall converse with St. Paul and all of the apostles, with the saints and martyrs, with all those Christians whose memory we honor, and with the great "shepherd and guardian of your souls," Jesus Christ (1 Pet. 2:25).

5. If you would not fear death, resign yourself to God's care. Suppose God should tell you to cast yourself into the sea, as Christ did to St. Peter (Matt. 14:18–29). Suppose He assures you that He will provide a fish to rescue you, as He did for Jonah (Jon. 1:17), or a port, or some other deliverance, security, or reward. Would you not be a most ungrateful and defiant person if you refused to act and thus obtain His blessing? The love of our own interest is a good antidote against fear. In forty or fifty years, we find evils enough in this life and arguments enough to make us weary of it. A good person knows many more reasons to be afraid of life than death, since death has less evil and more advantage.

6. If you would be unafraid of death, make no excuse to delay it, neither cover your fear with ingenious tasks to prolong your life. Some are not willing to submit to God's sentence of death until they have finished a certain design, or written the last paragraph of their book, or raised such portions of money for their children, or preached so many sermons, or built their house, or planted their orchard, or ordered their estate with such advantages. It is well for the modesty of these people that an excuse is ready; but if it were not, they would search one out.

Petronius describes Eumolpus composing verses in a desperate storm. Being forced to shift for himself when the ship is dashed upon the rocks, he cries out that he cannot deal with this until he has finished his verse. The fellow either had too strong a desire to end his verse or too great a desire not to end his life. But God's times are not to be measured by our circumstances; and what I value, God regards not. If my activity is truly essential, God will accomplish it with other contingencies of His providence.

If Epaphroditus had died when he had his great sickness (Phil. 2:25–27), God would have secured the work of the gospel without him. He also could have spared St. Stephen, St. Peter, as well as St. James. Say no more. When God calls, lay aside your papers. Dress your soul, then dress your hearse.

Blindness is odious, widowhood is sad, poverty is without comfort, persecution is full of trouble, famine is intolerable, and tears are the sad ease of a sadder heart. All of these are evils of life, not of death. Those who "die in the Lord" are so far from wanting the things of this life that they do not want life itself.

After all this, I do not say it is a sin to be afraid of death. The boldest human being may speak of it with confidence and dare to undertake a danger as big as death, yet shrink at the horror of death when it comes dressed in its proper circumstances. Our blessed Lord was pleased to legitimate our fears by His agony and prayers in the Garden (Luke 22:39–46). It is not a sin to be afraid, but it is a great joy to be without fear. Our Savior set aside that joy because it was agreeable to His purposes to suffer everything that we might suffer, everything but sin.

But when we strive by all means to avoid death, we are like those who by any means strive to be rich: They may blaspheme and dishonor God, engage in base sin, or curse God and die; but in all cases, they die. They die no less for their riches. To be angry with God, to quarrel with God, to defy His natural sentence of death, is an argument of huge folly and the parent of great trouble. Such a person is foolish to no purpose.

Fear can keep us in bondage all our lives, says St. Paul (Rom. 8:15). By contrast, patience enables us able to control our lives and come to possess what is in our best interest (Rom. 8:25). Therefore, as the Lord said, "In your patience possess ye your souls" (Luke 21:19, KJV), and you shall die with ease.

If all the parts of this discourse be true, if the promises of heaven be better than dreams, and if they be more than the vain dreams of deluded persons, then we should really desire death and account it among the good things of God. St. Paul understood this well when he desired that his "earthly tent" be "destroyed" (2 Cor. 5:1). He well enough knew his own advantages, and he pursued them accordingly, yet he was ready to leave them all behind.

It is certain that anyone who is afraid of death—I mean, with a violent and transporting fear, a fear that would betray one's duty or abandon one's patience—that person either loves this world too much or dares not trust God enough for the next.

13. Meditation on Death

Gerhard Groote

Unamuno, a noted Spanish philosopher of the twentieth century, makes this comment about our contemplation of death: "Although this meditation upon mortality may soon induce in us a sense of anguish, it fortifies us in the end. Retire, reader, into yourself and imagine a slow dissolution of yourself—the light dimming about you, all things becoming dumb and soundless, enveloping you in silence, the objects that you handle crumbling away between your hands, the ground slipping from under your feet, your memory vanishing as if in a swoon, everything melting away from you into nothingness and you yourself also melting away, the very consciousness of nothingness, merely as the phantom harborage of a shadow, not even remaining to you."[1]

---

[1]Miguel de Unamuno, *The Tragic Sense of Life* (New York: The Macmillan Company, 1921), 42.

Everyone has occasion to ponder the fact that we are earthly and temporal. But there is also a meditation in which we are convinced that our spiritual selves, instead of being mortal, are clothed with immortality and were intended for companionship with God throughout eternity. Moreover, we become aware that eternal life does not necessarily begin after the grave; it is lived in quality *now.*

Gerhard Groote, a leading Christian preacher in fourteenth-century Holland, had his preaching license revoked because of his criticism of organized religion. Retiring at his home at Deventer, he organized a Christian community known as the Brethren of the Common Life and spent the remaining year of his life writing much of *The Imitation of Christ.* Only a few months before his own death (caused by caring for an ill friend), he wrote these penetrating thoughts about death. His main theme is: Live eternal life *now* and you will have no fear about death.

Very quickly there will be an end of you here; realize therefore the impermanence of your human nature: Today you are, tomorrow you are gone.

Oh, the stupidity and hardness of the human heart, to think only upon the present and not care for what is to come!

You ought so to order yourself in all your thoughts and actions, as if today you were to die.

If you had a clear conscience, you would not greatly fear death.

It were better for you to avoid sin than to escape death.

If today you are not prepared, how will you be so tomorrow?

Tomorrow is uncertain, and how do you know that you shall live till tomorrow?

What is the point of living a long life, when there is so little change in us?

Alas! Length of days does not always better us, but often rather increases our sin.

Oh, that we had spent but one day in this world thoroughly well!

If we suppose death is dreadful, let us remember that to live long may prove more dangerous.

Happy is the one who always has the hour of death in mind and daily prepares to die.

When you see someone else die, take note that you must do the same.

When it is morning, reflect that you may die before night.

When evening comes, dare not to promise yourself the next morning.

Be therefore always in readiness, and so live that death may never catch you unprepared.

A perfect contempt of the world, a fervent desire to go forward in all virtue, a love of discipline, a laborious repentance, a ready obedience, a denying of self, and an endurance of any affliction whatsoever for the love of Christ—these will give us confidence that we shall die happily.

Time now is very precious. Now is the day of salvation; now is the accepted time.

God forbid that you spend time so idly here, in which you might obtain life eternal.

O beloved, from how great danger might you deliver yourself, from how great fear might you free yourself, if you would be ever fearful and mindful of death!

Labor to live so now that at the hour of death you may rejoice rather than fear.

Learn now to die to the world, so that you may begin to live with Christ.

Learn now to abandon all things, so that you may freely go to Christ.

Do these things now—even now, my beloved, to the fullest extent whatsoever you are able to do—for you do not know when you shall die or what shall befall you at the hour of death.

Now, while you have time, heap unto yourself everlasting riches.

Think on nothing but the salvation of your soul; care for nothing but the things of God.

Now honor the saints of God and imitate their actions, so that when you fail they may receive you into their everlasting fellowship.

Consider yourself a stranger and pilgrim upon the earth, who has nothing to do with the affairs of this world.

Keep your heart free and lifted up to God, because you have here no abiding city.

Send to Him your daily prayers and sighs, together with your tears, so that after death your spirit may be found worthy to pass into the presence of the Lord. *Amen.*

14. A Devout Prayer *and* A Meditation on God

Sir Thomas More

One of England's greatest lay statesmen was Thomas More. In 1529 he was made chancellor to King Henry VIII, the first layman to hold that position. To his lovely estate at Chelsea, More retired each Friday for prayer and meditation. He felt he needed deep contact with God if he was to offer sane advice to the king. The day came, however, when More would not sanction the king's marriage to Anne Boleyn, nor would he acknowledge King Henry VIII as the temporal head of the church. So More was imprisoned in the London Tower to await trial and punishment. On July 7, 1535, Thomas More was executed.

"A Devout Prayer" and "A Meditation on God" were written by Thomas More shortly before his death. Both are great devotional writings, showing how the saturation of a person's soul with the Spirit of God by daily spiritual discipline can give one courage to face death. Before we read these great prayers of Thomas More, let us put ourselves in his place. Note the trust he places in God's power and goodness. Observe how he united his will with that of God and yearned to be with Him. Especially notice More's rejoicing in Christ's presence as he waited for his execution.

We are living in the same universe with Thomas More. As we pray his prayers, let us meditate upon our eternal companionship with God and Christ, whether we remain here on this planet or begin our glorious adventure into eternity. Like Paul and Thomas More, we can say with surety, "Neither death, nor life . . . will be able to separate us from the love of God in Christ Jesus our Lord" (Rom. 8:38–39).

A Devout Prayer

Glorious God, give me Your grace to fix my heart so firmly upon You that I may say with Your blessed apostle Paul: "The world has been crucified to me, and I to the world" (Gal. 6:14). "For me, living is Christ and dying is gain" (Phil. 1:21). "My desire is to depart and be with Christ, for that is far better" (Phil. 1:23).

Give me Your grace to amend my life and to view my end without grudging. To them that die in You, good Lord, death is the gate to a wealthy life.

Almighty God, "Teach me to do your will" (Ps. 143:10). "Draw me after you" (Song 1:4). "Teach me your way, O Lord, and lead me on a level path because of my enemies" (Ps. 27:11). My "temper must be curbed with bit and bridle, else it will not stay near you" (Ps. 32:9).

O glorious God, take from me all sinful fear, all sinful sorrow and pensiveness, all sinful hope, all sinful mirth and gladness. Nonetheless give me such fear, such sorrow, such heaviness, such comfort, consolation, and gladness as shall be profitable for my soul: "Deal with your servant according to your steadfast love, and teach me your statutes" (Ps. 119:124).

Good Lord, give me the grace in all my fear and agony to remember that great fear and wonderful agony that You, my sweet Savior, had at the Mount of Olives before the most bitter Passion. In meditating thereon, allow me to conceive ghostly comfort and consolation profitable for my soul.

Almighty God, take from me all vainglorious thoughts and all appetite for my own praise. Remove all envy, covetousness, gluttony, sloth, and lechery; all wrath and appetite for revenge; all desire or delight of other folks' harm; all pleasure in provoking any person to wrath and anger; all delight of censure or insult against any person in their affliction and calamity.

And give me, good Lord, a mind that is humble, lowly, quiet, peaceable, patient, charitable, kind, tender, and full of pity. With all my works, all my words, and all my thoughts, give my life the taste of Your blessed Holy Spirit.

Give me, good Lord, a full faith, a firm hope, and a fervent charity. Inspire within me a love of the good Lord incomparably above the love of myself. Grant that I love nothing to Your displeasure, but everything in order to draw closer to You.

Give me, good Lord, a longing to be with You—not to avoid the calamities of this wretched world, nor to avoid the pains of purgatory, nor to escape the pains of hell, nor even to attain the joys of heaven—but for true love of You.

Take from me, good Lord, a lukewarm manner of meditation and dullness in praying unto You. Give me warmth, delight, and quickness in thinking upon You. Give me grace to long for Your holy sacraments, especially to rejoice in the presence of Your blessed body, sweet Savior Christ, in the holy sacrament of the altar. May I duly thank You for Your gracious visitation there. In all that high memorial, enable me to consider Your most bitter Passion.

Have mercy upon us, O Lord, have mercy on us. Let Your mercy, O Lord, be upon us, for we have hoped in You. In You, O Lord, have I hoped. Let me not be confounded forever.

A Meditation on God

    Give me grace, good Lord,
    To set the world at nothing
    And set my mind fast upon You,
    Hanging no longer upon the words of
      men's mouths.
    To be content with solitude,
    To long no more for human company,
    Little by little utterly to cast off the
      world
    And rid my mind of all the business
      thereof.
    To long no more for news of worldly
      things,
      But to feel displeasure, as if hearing
      silly dreams.
        To think gladly of God,
    To call piteously for His help,
        To lean upon God's comfort,
    To labor busily in loving Him.

    To know my vile and wretched nature,
      And to humble myself under the
      mighty hand of God.
    To bewail my sins past,
      For the purging of them
    Patiently to suffer adversity.
    Gladly to bear my purgatory here,
    To be joyful of tribulations,
    To walk the narrow way that leads to life,

And to bear the cross with Christ.
To have the last thing in remembrance,
    To have ever before my eye
My death, which is ever at hand,
To make death no stranger to me.
 To foresee and consider the everlasting
    fire of hell,
To pray for pardon before the Judge to
    come.
To have continually in mind
The Passion that Christ suffered for me,
    For His benefits incessantly to give
    Him thanks.
To redeem the time that I have lost,
To abstain from vain conversations,
To abandon light, foolish mirth and
    gladness,
To cut off unnecessary recreations.
Of worldly substance—
Friends, liberty, life, and all—
To consider their loss as nothing
For the winning of Christ.
To think my worst enemies my best
    friends,
For the brothers of Joseph could never
    have done him
So much good with their love and favor
As they did him with their malice and
    hatred.

15. The Luminous Trail

Rufus M. Jones

To face one's own death is a unique experience; to face the death of a loved one, especially that of a small child, can be a far more difficult experience. Rufus Jones's description of the death of his son Lowell stands as one of the most beautiful and deeply spiritual portrayals of victorious living.[1] As a teacher at Haverford College for a half century and the writer of more than fifty books on spiritual values, Rufus Jones the Quaker stood as one of America's finest religious leaders.

Rufus Jones's experience will add confidence that in such events one's religion is something to *use*, not *lose*. One can appreciate Jones's

---

[1]Rufus M. Jones, *The Luminous Trail* (New York: Macmillan Company, 1947), 164–165.

observation that in such an experience, "love can span this break of separation, can pass beyond the visible and hold right on across the chasm."

If we share Jesus' teaching that God is our Father, we share His assurance that God is ever to be trusted and that His fatherhood spans throughout eternity. Said Jesus, "If you then, who are evil, know how to give good gifts to your children, how much more will your Father in heaven give good things to those who ask him!" (Matt. 7:11).

All too soon this boy, "by the vision splendid on his way attended," came to an end here on earth where I could see him. He had diphtheria in the spring of 1903. He was given antitoxin and recovered, as far as we could see, completely. In July I went to England to lecture in the Quaker Summer School, which was to be the opening of the Woodbrooke Settlement at Selly Oak, near Birmingham. Lowell was to stay at his grandmother's home in Ardonia, New York, with a very efficient Friend who was to be caretaker and companion. He was always happy at Ardonia, with aunts and cousins, and we left feeling very comfortable about him. But the night before landing in Liverpool I awoke in my berth with a strange sense of trouble and sadness. As I lay wondering what it meant, I felt myself invaded by a Presence and held by Everlasting Arms. It was the most extraordinary experience I had ever had. But I had no intimation that anything was happening to Lowell. When we landed in Liverpool a cable informed me that he was desperately ill, and a second cable, in answer to one from me, brought the dreadful news that he was gone. When the news reached my friend John Wilhelm Rowntree, he experienced a profound sense of Divine Presence enfolding him and me, and his comfort and love were an immense help to me in my trial. Philip Wicksteed, the great Dante and Wordsworth scholar, gave me unique help in that early darkness, and he became one of my guides to St. Francis of Assisi, and to the triumph of love.

There had mysteriously come to Lowell an attack of paralysis that affected his speech and his breathing. He seems to have fully realized that he could not live long, and he wrote on a slip of paper: "Give some of my books to Philip and Norris"—two of his dearest friends at Haverford. His little friends and playmates later joined together and raised a memorial fund and finished and furnished "The Lowell Jones Reading Room" in the Boys' School at Ramallah, Palestine. Lowell's picture hangs in this attractive room, and Arabic boys have carried on a happy memory of him.

All of a sudden, as the end came, he raised his hands in wonder and got voice enough to say, "Oh, Mother," as though they had found each other in the world that is Real, for this boy undoubtedly belonged to the kingdom of God. Julian of Norwich, who never had a child, said: "To me was shown no higher stature than child-hood." I knew exactly how Emerson felt when he wrote "Threnody," when he had lost his boy:

> There's not a sparrow or a wren,
> There's not a blade of autumn grain,
> Which the four seasons do not tend
> And tides of life and increase lend;
> And every chick and every bird,
> And weed and rock-moss is preferred.
> O ostrich-like forgetfulness!
> O loss of larger in the less!
> Was there no star that could be sent,
> No watcher in the firmament,
> No angel from the countless host
> That loiters round the crystal coast,
> Could stoop to heal that only child,
> Nature's sweet marvel undefiled,
> And keep the blossoms of the earth,
> Which all her harvests were not worth?

I know now, as I look back across the years, that nothing has carried me up into the life of God or done more to open out the infinite mean-ing of love than the fact that love can span this break of separation, can pass beyond the visible and hold right on across the chasm. The mystic union has not broken and knows no end. Lowell had here only eleven years of happy, joyous life. The victory that comes through the long years of struggle in a world full of hard choices could not be his. He was not to have the chance, "with toil of heart and knees and hands, through the long gorge to the far light," to form his character and to do his lifework; but who knows what chances there are for transplanted human worth to bloom, to profit in God's other garden?

As certainly as God lives there is more to follow after this brief span of preparation ends. Those who are only potential saints here — "probable" saints — may very well become full-fledged shining ones when God has brought the beginning to its complete fulfillment. When my sorrow was at its most acute stage, I was walking along a great city highway when suddenly I saw a little child come out of a great gate that swung to and fastened behind her. She wanted to go to her home behind the gate, but it would not open. She pounded in vain with her little fist. She rattled the gate. Then she wailed as though her heart would break. The cry brought the mother. She caught the child in her arms and kissed away the tears. "Didn't you know I would come? It is all right now." All of a sudden I saw with my spirit that there was love behind my shut gate.

Yes, "where there is so much love, *there must be more.*"

16. A Meditation for Evening

Lancelot Andrewes

Lancelot Andrewes, bishop of the Church of England at Chichester, Ely, and Winchester in the seventeenth century, was a close friend of King James I. He was one of the rare linguists of his day, being master of fifteen languages, and helped to translate the King James Version of the Bible published in 1611. However, Bishop Andrewes will be most remembered for his *Private Devotions,* one of the richest devotional classics of Christendom. Written privately for his own use, in the Latin and Greek languages, it was translated into English and released to the public shortly after Andrewes's death in 1626.

The basis of *Private Devotions* is a set of seven devotional patterns, to be used for each of the seven days of the week. For each of these days,

Andrewes wrote meditations upon the following themes: Meditation, Adoration, Confession of Sin, Prayer for Grace, Confession of Faith, Intercession, and Thanksgiving. The total pattern of prayer, with its main note on one's penitence and concern for the sins of the world, enriches the self to face both life and death.

Within the pages of *Private Devotions* are other prayers, especially meditations for morning and evening. The prayer that follows sees the analogy of evening time and the late days of life. To read this prayer is to discern Andrewes's humility and contrition, his absolute dependence on God, and his belief that prayer is a kind of incense that cleanses the life of the worshiper. Prayer reminds a person that life is wholly dependent upon God, whose grace will arm us in every experience, even death itself.

> The day is gone,
> and I give Thee thanks, O Lord.
> Evening is at hand,
> make it bright unto us.
> As day has its evening,
> so also has life;
> the even of life is age,
> age has overtaken me,
> make it bright unto us.
> Cast me not away in the time of age;
> forsake me not when my strength faileth me.

Even to my old age be Thou He,
and even to hoar hairs carry me;
do Thou make, do Thou bear,
do Thou carry and deliver me.

Abide with me, Lord,
for it is toward evening,
and the day is far spent
of this fretful life.
Let Thy strength be made perfect
in my weakness.

Day is fled and gone,
life too is going,
this lifeless life.
Night cometh,
and cometh death,
the deathless death.
Near as is the end of day,
so too is the end of life:
We then, also remembering it,
beseech of Thee
for the close of our life,
that Thou wouldst direct it in peace,
Christian, acceptable,
sinless, shameless,
and, if it please Thee, painless,
Lord, O Lord,
gathering us together
under the feel of Thine Elect,

when Thou wilt, and as Thou wilt,
only without shame and sins.
Remember we to outstrip the night
doing some good thing.
By night I lift up my hands in the sanctuary,
and praise the Lord.
The Lord hath granted His
    loving-kindness
in the daytime;
and in the night season did I sing of Him,
and made my prayer unto the God of my
    life.
As long as I live I will magnify Thee on
    this manner
and lift up my hands in Thy Name.
Let my prayer be set forth in Thy sight
as the incense,
and let the lifting up of my hands
be an evening sacrifice.
Blessed art Thou, O Lord, our God,
the God of our fathers,
who hast created the changes of days and
    nights,
who givest songs in the night,
who hast delivered us from the evil of
    this day,
who hast not cut off like a weaver my life,
nor from day even to night made an end
    of time.

17. Looking at Death through the Poets' Eyes

BE NOT AFRAID
Walt Whitman

> We too take ship, O soul.
> Joyous we too launch out on trackless
>   seas . . .
> Caroling free, singing our song of God,
> Chanting our chant of pleasant explora-
>   tion . . .
> Sail forth — steer for the deep waters
>   only,
> Reckless, O soul, exploring, I with thee,
>   and thou with me,
> For we are bound where the mariner has
>   not yet dared to go,
> And we will risk the ship, ourselves and
>   all.

O my brave soul!
O farther, farther sail!
O daring joy but safe! are they not all the
    seas of God?
O farther, farther, farther sail!

DEATH STANDS ABOVE ME
Walter Savage Landor

Death stands above me, whispering low
I know not what into my ear:
Of his strange language all I know
Is, there is not a word of fear.

WELL DONE
James Montgomery

Servant of God, well done!
Rest from thy loved employ:
The battle fought, the victory won,
Enter thy Master's joy.

The pains of death are past,
Labor and sorrow cease,
And Life's long warfare closed at last,
Thy soul is found in peace.

SELFISHNESS
Margaret E. Bruner

>Death takes our loved one—
>>We are bowed in grief. For whom?
>Are we not selfish?
>A mourner weeps for himself,
>The dead know nought of sorrow.

O HAPPY SOUL
Washington Gladden

>O happy soul, be thankful now, and rest!
>Heaven is a goodly land;
>And God is love; and those he loves are
>>blest;
>Now thou dost understand
>The least thou hast is better than the best
>That thou didst hope for; now upon thine
>>eyes
>The new life opens fair;
>Before thy feet the blessed journey lies
>Through homelands everywhere;
>And heaven to thee is all a sweet sur-
>>prise.

IF MY BARK SINK
Emily Dickinson

> If my bark sink
> 'Tis to another sea.
> Mortality's ground floor
> Is immortality.

THE EARTH IS FULL
OF GOD'S GOODNESS
James Montgomery

> If God hath made this world so fair,
> Where sin and death abound,
>   How beautiful, beyond compare,
>   Will paradise be found!

DEATH
Thomas May

> The wisest men are glad to die; no fear
> Of death can touch a true philosopher.
> Death sets the soul at liberty to fly.

LORD! IT IS NOT LIFE TO LIVE
Augustus M. Toplady

> Lord! it is not life to live,
> If Thy presence Thou deny;

Lord! if Thou Thy presence give,
'Tis no longer death—to die.

Source and Giver of repose,
Singly from Thy smile it flows;
Peace and happiness are Thine;
Mine they are, if Thou art mine.

THE ETERNAL GOODNESS
John Greenleaf Whittier

Yet, the maddening maze of things,
And tossed by storm and flood,
To one fixed trust my spirit clings;
I know that God is good!

. . . .

I know not what the future hath
Of marvel or surprise,
Assured alone that life and death
His mercy underlies.

. . . .

I know not where His islands lift
Their fronded palms in air;
I only know I cannot drift
Beyond His love and care.

O LOVE THAT WILT NOT LET ME GO
George Matheson

> O Love that wilt not let me go,
> I rest my weary soul in Thee;
> I give Thee back the life I owe,
> That in Thine ocean depths its flow
> May richer, fuller be.
>
> O Light that followest all my way,
> I yield my flickering torch to Thee;
> My heart restores its borrowed ray,
> That in Thy sunshine's blaze its day,
> May brighter, fairer be.
>
> O Joy that seekest me through pain,
> I cannot close my heart to Thee;
> I trace the rainbow through the rain,
> And feel the promise is not vain
> That morn shall tearless be.
>
> O Cross that liftest up my head,
> I dare not ask to fly from Thee;
> I lay in dust life's glory dead,
> And from the ground there blossoms red
> Life that shall endless be.

18. Looking at Death through Great Prayers

FOR GOD'S SAFE KEEPING
St. Patrick

May the strength of God pilot us. May the power of God preserve us. May the wisdom of God instruct us. May the hand of God protect us. May the way of God direct us. May the shield of God defend us. May the host of God guard us against the snares of the Evil One and the temptations of the world. May Christ be with us. Christ before us. Christ in us. Christ over us. May Thy salvation, O Lord, be always ours this day and for evermore. *Amen.*

MAY GOD BE IN MY HEAD
Sarah Primer (1558)

> God be in my head,
> And in my understanding;
>
> God be in my eyes
> And in my looking;
>
> God be in my mouth
> And in my speaking;
>
> God be in my heart
> And in my thinking;
>
> God be at my end,
> And at my departing.

TO RELAX IN SLEEP
WITH PEACE AT NIGHT
Thomas Dee

Heavenly Father, we commit ourselves to Thee; take us into Thy care this night. Cause us to lie down in peace and to rise in safety; let no evil come nigh us, nor plague about our dwelling. Defend us from all the terrors of night; let not evil have any power over us to hurt us, but be Thou ever near — yea, close to us, in our souls, and bodies, and our dwelling. Be Thou the subject of our sleeping and waking thoughts, that when we awake, whether it be in this life or the next, we may still be with Thee. Cause us to lie down to sleep in the hope that, should we not awake again in this life, we may awake and rise in the morning of our Redeemer's coming in His Kingdom.

And should we awake again here, grant that our souls may be enlightened by Thy Spirit, as our bodies by the returning sun. Be Thou the first object of our awakening thoughts and through the coming day. Enable us to keep it holy, not doing our own ways, nor finding our own pleasures, nor speaking our own words, but walking in Thy way; through Jesus Christ Thy Son, our Savior. *Amen.*

REST FROM A TROUBLED WORLD
W.E. Orchard

Wearied by the conflict of life, worn by the burden of the day, we seek Thee as our resting place. May Thy eternal calm descend upon our troubled spirits and give us all Thy peace. Amid the treacherous sands of time Thou standest still, the Rock of Ages. In life's desert places Thou, O Christ, art a spring whose waters never fail; hear us, we beseech Thee, O Lord Christ. *Amen.*

WE ARE THINE, O GOD
Bishop Gilbert Burnet

And now, O God, we turn our thoughts wholly from the world and all worldly objects to look upon Thee. Thou hast dealt hitherto with us so preciously that we cannot mistrust Thy Providence but cast ourselves wholly upon Thee. We dedicate ourselves afresh to Thee. Give us the joys of Thy salvation. Let us find that whatever trials Thou dost put us to Thou art with us.

Lead us, if Thou wilt, through the valley of the shadow of death, for even there Thou art with us. Bring us at last where Thou art, O God, and our All. We are Thine, O our God, do with us what seems good in Thy sight — our God and our Portion forever. *Amen.*

GIVE THY SERVANTS OF THYSELF
John Neale

> O Give Thy servants patience to be still
> and hear Thy will;
> Courage to venture wholly on Thine arm
> that will not harm;
> The wisdom that will never let us stray
> out of our way;
> The love that now afflicting

knoweth best when we should rest..
Amen.

PSALM 90

Lord, you have been our dwelling
place
   in all generations.
Before the mountains were brought
forth,
   or ever you had formed the earth
   and the world,
from everlasting to everlasting you are
God.

You turn us back to dust,
   and say, "Turn back, you mortals."
For a thousand years in your sight
   are like yesterday when it is past,
   or like a watch in the night.

You sweep them away; they are like a
dream,
   like grass that is renewed in the
   morning;
in the morning it flourishes and is
renewed;
   in the evening it fades and withers.

All our days pass away under your
wrath;
    our years come to an end like a sigh.
The days of our life are seventy years,
    or perhaps eighty, if we are strong;
even then their span is only toil and
trouble;
    they are soon gone, and we fly
    away.

. . . .

Let your work be manifest to your
servants,
    and your glorious power to their
    children.
Let the favor of the Lord our God be
upon us,
    and prosper for us the work of our
    hands—
    O prosper the work of our hands!

19. Looking at Death through the Words of Christ

If any want to become my followers, let them deny themselves and take up their cross and follow me. For those who want to save their life will lose it, and those who lose their life for my sake will find it. For what will it profit them if they gain the whole world but forfeit their life? Or what will they give in return for their life?

— Matthew 16:24–26

Everyone who has left houses or brothers or sisters or father or mother or children or fields, for my name's sake, will receive a hundredfold, and will inherit eternal life.

— Matthew 19:29

Indeed they cannot die anymore, because they are like angels and are children of God, being children of the resurrection. And the fact that the dead are raised Moses himself showed, in the story about the [burning] bush, where he speaks of the Lord as the God of Abraham, the God of Isaac, and the God of Jacob. Now he is God not of the dead, but of the living; for to him all of them are alive.

— Luke 20:36–38

Just as Moses lifted up the serpent in the wilderness, so must the Son of Man be lifted up, that whoever believes in him may have eternal life. For God so loved the world that he gave his only Son, so that everyone who believes in him may not perish but may have eternal life.

— John 3:14–16

Very truly, I tell you, anyone who hears my word and believes him who sent me has eternal life, and does not come under judgment, but has passed from death to life.

Very truly, I tell you, the hour is coming, and is now here, when the dead will hear the voice of the Son of God, and those who hear will live. For just as the Father has life in himself, so he has granted the Son also to have life in himself; and he has given him authority to execute judgment, because he is the Son of Man. Do not be astonished at this; for the hour is coming when all who are in their graves will hear his voice and will come out—those who have done good, to the resurrection of life, and those who have done evil, to the resurrection of condemnation.

— John 5:24–29

My sheep hear my voice. I know them, and they follow me. I give them eternal life, and they will never perish. No one will snatch them out of my hand.

— John 10:27–28

I am the resurrection and the life. Those who believe in me, even though they die, will live, and everyone who lives and believes in me will never die. Do you believe this?

— John 11:25–26

Be faithful unto death, and I will give you the crown of life.

— Revelation 2:10c